White Rose Bards

A Yorkshire UK Poetry Anthology

Edited by
James P. Wagner (Ishwa)

White Rose Bards

Copyright © 2020 by Local Gems Press

www.localgemspoetrypress.com

Buzzin Bards Yard President:

Benjamin William Crisafulli (Ushiku)

Bards International President:

James P. Wagner (Ishwa)

Dedicated to all poets in the Yorkshire, U.K. area!

Foreword

Yorkshire has a fine tradition of literature from the Old English poetry of Cædmon to the beautiful prose of the Bronte Sisters, and so when Local Gems asked "where to next?" the answer was obvious. Living Mossley-way I'm just a short bus ride from Saddleworth, while one sister was married in Bradford and the other went to Uni in Leeds and now lives in Keighley.

Yorkshire's just one of them places that has something for everyone. Football? Check. Rugby? No problem. Music? Riotous! Food? Tha'll be having a belly full of Yorkshire pudding. History? Romans, Vikings, and a certain White Rose all come to mind. It's the largest and most diverse county with beautiful moorlands and vibrant cities and is a place where past and present don't just collide, they're very much alive.

The physical launch was sadly postponed due to the Lockdown, but in typical Yorkshire fashion the hunger to just get on with it was there (as emails would attest). So I suggested an online launch – offering the dozens of incredible poets that feature in our first of many White Rose Bards anthologies the chance to perform and record their poems digitally. But rest assured that as soon as large gatherings are allowed again we'll get to hear your beautiful words in person.

~ Benjamin William Crisafulli (Ushiku)

Table of Contents

Robert Bates

Winter

When snow begins descending onto ploughed fields,
where the air is crisp,
hedgerows become silver lace.
There I stand and I listen
to the sweet songs of small birds.

Robert Bates is currently studying an undergraduate degree at the University of York where he has performed in a number of poetry recitals and contemporary art installations. He has experimented with different poetic forms from traditional Japanese to concrete and sound poetry, and he is currently researching and translating the works of Soviet poets.

Andy Carrington

Unskilled Labourer Has Loadsa Jobs

Hard work don't
pay

if it did, show me rich donk-ey?

not a Dogsbody who does as a Dogs-
body does: the most
work
@ the opposite end of the food
chain (go
figure)

another Jack-of-all-trades / master of none

grafting for peanuts

making stars outta the super-
iors

they always take the piss

would much rather do a BUKOWSKI and drink in the booze-
r

not stressing bout rent over-
due / factotum / swinging from role-to-
role
on temp contracts

another part-time slave doing full-time work / another
/ having to do the crap jobs no 1 else wants to
do

1st 1 to arrive / last 1 out the door

picking up banana skins / washing-
up the plates / scrubbing skid marks
off the
bogs

always cleaning up after people

taking the
lip
when things go wrong
or anything goes missing

    ALL TO PAY THE BILLS
the Proletarian puts his / her [equal-

opportunity] arse on the
line
to pay for a week's shopping in
wages
just trying to make an honest
living
while the Band 7ers never make eye
contact

leaving half-
drunk cups of peppermint
tea
@ their decks

pushing pencils / scrolling through their e-
mails / buying
shite
off ETSY / planning weekends away to CENTER
PARCS with Gran / Granddaddy & the

kids.

I guess I'll do it, then?

Andy Carrington is DIY a Punk-Poet from Bradford

Ella Christian-Sims

Yorkshire puddings for breakfast

I feel heat wrapping around my eyeballs,
I wonder if they'll thaw.

She says "we should light a candle"
charred temples close my eyes.

I wonder if she lights candles
Because she misses her ex-husband,
Tea in the conservatory,
Poirot on a night,
Bill Bryson read incessantly before a trip;

Or if guilt has set up camp in her chest
She can feel it building foundations,
Pulmonary artery clogged by greed and vicious affairs.
Maybe she thinks her knees might buckle,
If not for a Christian donation.

her candle is lit and she makes her prayer
(her eyes on me instead of the flame).

And she turns to me and says that I am *"too young*
To have had people die quite yet".
I light my candle,
Wonder how quickly the church blows them out,
Ready for someone else's dead person.

I want to sit and think about my nights slept with the
light on,
tepid water, a bathroom so grayscale I thought the life had
been removed,
The day the sun wasn't given to me
My friend who stopped my hands from shaking, destroyed.

I want to stay and watch my memory turn from ice
to soup,
But she wants to tell me about Yorkshire puddings for
breakfast.
A conversation that takes an hour,
And then moves onto haggis.
She tells me this is her favourite church
I think about reminding her of her atheism,
But then remind me of mine.

Ella Christian-Sims is an aspiring poet from North Yorkshire, a commended foyle young poet 2018. She is currently studying English literature with creative writing at Newcastle University. She has had short poems published in online magazines, mostly based around the topics of feminism or politics.

Bill Clayton

It's A Snake's Life

A young snake slithered up to his dad,
To ask a question that bothered the lad
"I've often wondered what sort we are
You know – what kind of snake
Do we wrap ourselves round people
Till their bones begin to break?

Do we not stop, till their eyes go pop,
Or do we just scare them to death,
Do we swallow them whole
Or just grab a hold
Till we squeeze out all of their breath?

Are we the sort of stripey kind
That blend in with the trees,
Or the slimey, slippy greasy lot
That brings them to their knees?

Or dad, are we them poisonous snakes
That kill with just one bite.
I've never been sure, if there's really a cure
But I've often hoped there might."

The big old snake opened up one eye,
And looked down at the youth
And wondered why,
There was a tear in his eye,
And a gap where there once was a tooth.

The sleepy dad, wondered why his lad
Looked so worried for one so young,
He had no doubt, when the boy shouted out
"I've gone and bit me tongue ! "

Bill Clayton started his Word Doodling at school, and his poetry reflects his time in the military as well as civilian life. Although not shown here, a number highlight his dealing with the illness Myalgic Encephalomyelitis (M.E.)

Peter Donnelly

New Season, Old City

When the daffodils begin to flower
on the city walls and Clifford's Tower,
croci bloom in the Museum Gardens
and frost no longer hardens
the land where I walk,
I know it is spring in York.
Treasurer's House will soon be
open, Beningbrough Hall is already.
The Christmas lights have at last come down,
on a weekend you can move in town.
In my flat the amaryllis bud appears
against lilac curtains like a ship in the sea
or a rocket in space
about to flame.

Peter Donnelly lives in York. He has degrees in English and Creative Writing from the University of Wales Lampeter. He has been writing poetry for twenty years and has been published in the South Bank Magazine and the the Ripon Poetry Festival Anthology 'Seeing Things' as well as The League of Poets 'Songs of Peace' anthology.

Ence

Sunshine

He was right there where I left him
surrounded by toys
Ongoing research, always hungry for more
Sensation of the landscape escaping from frame
My classic with a twist, half me

He gave me this smile
when he finds something sparkling enough
blast of new figure added to an old draft

He said mommy I know why Space has its name
It is so big everyone will find place there
Small sound in a large silence surrounded by time
Everything fits in everlasting shine

I brought him his favourite fruits
Bowl universe of apple planets and tangerine moons
The day was ending
There will be more twists soon

Ence is a restless spirit, she can be lawyer, fashion designer, transport planner, cleaner or bartender... but most of all Word Hunter. Surrounded by books, magazines, notes.. After many years of searching finally found her home at York.

Vivien Firth

My Visit to the Holocaust Museum

I stood within the vortex of the entrance of Yad Vashem
My eyes transfixed upon a lady waving to me from way
back when?
A brown cattle truck seemed packed with arms and hands
outstretched
But one lady's face and hands had me totally bewitched.

Was I being invited on a journey with no end
Or could I detect some disaster just around the bend?
My feet seemed set in concrete, as the truck was about to
leave
And yet I saw the waving hand and the eyes that seemed to
plead.

My heart was wrenched with longing and tears began
to flow
Was it some mother's darling daughter or a friend I used
to know?
I could feel the train moving as if I was on the track
Body swaying mechanically from side to side not able
to go back!

14

Suddenly I was shaken, back to reality's door
With the realisation my friends were not here with me as
before.
The horror of that journey that six million Jews had made
And I was just at the beginning of miseries cavalcade.

In silence I moved slowly into the corridors of time
Sensing and seeing suffering of the most horrendous kind
Children's shoes discarded, piled high in a heap
The tortured bodies of so many made my spirit weep.

Mangled spectacles formed another mountain rare
With skeletal faces and sunken eyes of dark despair
Endless horrors of betrayal, blackened hearts that knew no
shame
Tireless, tormentors, treating women as fair game.

One and half million children meeting an untimely death
Gassed, choked and smothered till they had no breath
Bright yellow stars of David lie contorted in muddied
ground
Once a mark of identification now an incinerated
blackened mound.

By now my heart is longing to breath fresh air again
To step beyond the confines of agony, shame and pain,
As if someone had heard my whispering beyond the evil

machinations
I arrive at a concrete circle surrounded by the Righteous
among the Nations

The circle became a well for me where I could let go of
the tears
Which had been locked up it seemed forever, beyond time
less years
I could see a light at the end of the tunnel and feel the
breeze blow
But this could not erase the memory of those remembered
from long ago

James Flynn

Infant Hercules

Infant Hercules that built the world fitfully
sleeping body furled
The time is nigh to give him a nudge
Make him aware of the need to budge
Alert him to the peril within
Tell him a fight back must begin
Founding Fathers Bolckow and Vaughn
Silently gaze on their Protege forlorn
Powerless to ease his sickly demise
Watching him fade before their eyes
Inwardly churning with dismay
Seeing his industrial life blood seep away
Dorman, Hustler, Sadler, Bell
Unable to quell the infants death knell
Bridge and Ship Building long gone
Mighty Steel hanging on
ICI long decamped parcelled up sold off revamped
Employment levels downward ramped
China sneezes Hercules wheezes
Redcar steel production freezes
Government non intervention appalling

Steely in resisting soft mothballing
Cabinet displaying metal fatigue
Chancellor obsessed with Chinese intrigue
Coke Ovens cooling inwardly crumbling
Blast Furnace survival hopes tumbling
Liquidator signalling an assets grab
Steel destined for the Mortuary Slab
Ships anchored off Redcar shore
Laden with life blood of coal and ore
Residents of Teesside rise as one
Lay siege to Parliament until the culprits are gone
Save the infant from the final rites
Confront the Chancellor and his Acolytes.

James Flynn is a Middlesbrough born septuagenarian, retired decorator who has had a lifelong interest in all sport and literature. In his youth he participated in cricket and football and is a lover of musical theatre. He started writing in verse approximately nine years ago.

Siobhan Gifford

Mother is a Verb

Buffeted by a shrill westerly
on a Heathcliff moor, bearings lost
in compost of fog; deep bog under foot,
dense cloudswirls blot the sooty mire,
ghostly views behind darkened hues.
A grouse croaks at my anxious feet,
sour fear oozes from deadened peat.

Where is he now, my Lyke Wake Walker?
My son, adrift on rank marshland,
just dim shapes of howes and tumuli
for pie-in-the-sky navigation
on a Yorkshire ocean of deep dank moss.

Has he passed Raven Stones, Blue Man i' th' Moss,
or is he lost on the tops at Shunner Howe?
Has he reached Fat Betty,
limestone boulder? Eyeless face
on stony shoulder.
A coin on her head wards off dread quagmire sprites.
On steepled bluff, the stench of fright.

Dirgers cross from east to west on coffin trails
that flail sumps and dales.
I scour the fog for my boy, his dog.
Phantom thoughts opaque the slough,
spectre worries in moorland rough.

Then cloud lifts the hem of its soggy blanket
for a signpost of sun on a far-flung thicket
and there at last,
three hours past deadline,
the grouse and I spot a hound, a head,
our quarry Lazarusing
from imagined dead.

Siobhan Gifford lives in the shadow of the famous White Horse of Kilburn on the edge of the North York Moors. A mosaicist, she also loves the puzzle of fitting words together to make a picture come alive with colour and emotion. She has been studying Creative Writing as part of an Arts and Humanities degree.

Rachel Glass

A Letter From Gran To Grandpa

It's been a decade or several millennia
since
and now,
I hold our love
in the palm of my hand:
less hurricane, more teacup.

Sometimes, loose threads
find their way to my sleeve
the way mountains find their way
to my front porch;
I can't explain how they got there

and I can't remember your chair
being anything but empty.
It has shrunk to the size of a cup

and your favourite cup has shrunk
to the size of a thimble
and I can't explain why.

Consider our beginning:

a clumsy wink
and a crooked smile,
an eyelash of a moment.

In our garden, there is a pile of bricks
where a bridge could
not stretch between us.

Without you, I am so, so tired,
my fingers far too frail
to rebuild our life.

Tell me Heaven is
less pearly gates,
more teapot.
You know I won't come
if there isn't any tea.

Rachel Glass lives in Scarborough and has been writing poetry since she was sixteen. Her poem 'Octopus' was highly commended in the 2020 Yaffle Poetry Competition. She can be found writing, drinking hot chocolate and wearing glittery shoes.

Richard Harries

The Shadow Box

As she lay dying
She looked up and saw
The shadow box of her life
The little things that mattered
The first ornament her boy had made at school
A souvenir from the seaside
Tiny shiny things
Nothing of value

Her life had been good and long
She had memories to look back on

She sighed and breathed her last

Time stood still
Then the house was cleared
Memories gone

And the shadow box?
Sadly.. on a bonfire smouldering

Then gone

Richard Harries is a Yorkshire poet who appears extensively at festivals and events throughout the North of England. He is 68 years of age and has been writing poetry for nine years. He has his first Anthology of poetry being published by Stairwell Books of York in January 2021. He has an internet presence with his YouTube channel rcpoems having scored over 130,000 views so far.

Kevin Heads

Designer child

He or she can have dark hair or blonde
I can change it all with my editing wand
Genetic sorcery a DNA twist
Write what you'd like on your shopping list

Tall or short you decide
A designer child to walk by your side
We can irradicate illness
All that we find
Strong of heart peace of mind

Maybe a girl
Blonde hair with the slightest curl
Slim and pretty
Dressed in pink
A future doctor, lawyer or shrink

Or a boy
Handsome and dark
A better version of his patriarch
Clever witty strong and bold

What a wonderful gift
For a mother to hold

How about twins exactly the same
From tip to the toe with similar brains
The perfect reflection no mirror required
Artistic perfection yet science inspired

The price is fair less for a pair
And insurance too for the aftercare
Not that you need it for defects are rare
And if it breaks
We have plenty of spares

Kevin Heads is now a full time writer of poetry and historical fiction. His poetry ranges across many subjects from nature and history to politics and technology. Nothing is off limits and his followers love the way he transports them to places and makes them consider and explore thoughts and emotions. Some of his poetry can be dark and frightning and these are extremely popular with his followers. I hope you like them too.

Richard Jenkins

Who is that 1 a.m ghost?

Everyone is working off their debt
And I'm still craving my bed
No , I don't suppose
It means much to you
Who stole the pitch
Put out the fire with a fiend of itch
Who took out the glimmer
Forced and plunged in the dimmer
Switch
In my sunbeam ?
I know, I know
It wasn't me or you
How to keep the fight and glee
And remove the raging part
Of my bronze heart
No
It wasn't you or me
And yet
Here is the sorrow
The metallic taste I could never
Stomach or swallow

Fine, fine I'll shut up
I've sold my stories for a cheap imitation
Of what used to be my most prized possession
No more colours left to lease to imagination
Yes, yes I see your eyes
turn to myopic flood
With the mist of apathies blood
My stories reek of an infection
I was once able to resist its detention
Dance away from
Now stumble , trip
Far from the starlit kiss of hips

This copper clipped bard found his vibe when he hit the rails.
From Manchester to Acomb. April 2019 was the beginning.
Dreaming of gothic grins. Catching sultry photons in the
Groves at twilight the bard scrawled , gems of fiery
hieroglyphics, Jewels of graffiti in darker shades.
Trinkets that simmer with the joy of bad habits but my hope
is they glimmer, winking merrily in the void of time. Above
all, my desire is that my poems provide a cinematic reel for
your minds projector.

Louis Kasatkin

Metropolis

Stark geometric lines
intersecting clean marble
and steel;
horizonless concourses
deserted entrance halls,
empty corridors
vacant escalators
ascending,
descending
in relentless
progression;
Walls hyphenated
with reminders
to purchase,
to consume
bellowing mutely
into the void;
shimmering platform mirrors,
clipped automated announcements,
data screens streaming
their silent prophecies;

Inexorable arrivals
whooshing
and rumbling,
debouching into
the gleaming Now
of a glass-towered
morning amid its
awakening rage
there on
the bench
face down,
his skin again
punctured,
no-one.

Louis Kasatkin is the editorial admin of
http://www.destinypoets.co.uk. His work has been
published, by amongst others, Medusa's Kitchen, Schlock! and
the Galway Review. A political and community activist and
blogger, others have referred to him as being a nuisance to the
status quo.

Rose E Kirby

Weather

The heady wind is
Boiling, coming up to the window for a gentle millisecond
of a sweet soft serenade before the harsh brute force of
rejection
Bubbling like the empath, under weights of darker skies
and lead balloons falling like a reverse "IT" scene, the
helium from the sewer lifting up to the sky and
plummeting again
Because it's cyclical, all of it, the quick, drip, trip of a
rainy puddle fall and the quick, slip, nip of a needle to the
burgeoning vein
Below the surface of a tantrum and a pore the intricate
bodies working, like the wind, pressing gently to caress,
and then the outpouring the outcry of furious trauma rears
its ugly head and
Being is no longer your journey. You are not being you.
Caught up in the wind carried to the heights of balloons to
fall like lead
Babbling lead droplets of weighted trauma recycled
through you, through each session each outcry
But will I get better?
But will WE get better?

But are we MEANT to?

Be.

B.

R E Kirby (Rose) is a passionate 22 year old Literature Graduate, lover and eclectic reader. Born to a Mam from Bradford, Yorkshire is her current place of residence, and her true home. God's Own Country, the Yorkshire Rose (perhaps her name's origin) and a good cuppa Yorkshire tea complement her avid writing of life and empathy.

Maria Grazia Lucrezia Leotta

Back to Life
(a poem for Richard III)

I can hear the clash of swords and halberds
I see him, he will be mine.
I go straight towards my target
I need to do it for my people, my kingdom, my crown
nothing is lost yet.

My horse runs, the drum in my chest beats fast
my breath warms my face under the helmet,
this is my moment.
The noise of the battle is roaring for me
my knights are ready
the White Boar will win. Again.

Suddenly my horse stops, I fall down
I need to fight on my feet.
Soldiers are waiting for me in the storm of the battle
They look at me, I look in their eyes
but hatred and rage burn in them,
I can see the fire of treachery.

Alone. I feel alone
the clash of swords and halberds is against me now.
I fight with all my strength against my assailants.
Something enters my body,
I feel the acute pain of metal inside my flesh
I am falling, my helmet is lost, nothing can save me now.
All is lost.

The White Rose is losing her petals,
something warm and red is covering my face
I can taste blood in my mouth
the White Boar can't win anymore
betrayal is murdering him.
My crown is lost, my kingdom is lost, life is
abandoning me.
Treason! Oh Lord, save my soul.

Silence and darkness.
The noise of the battle is distant now.
 I can't hear it anymore.
I see my naked body viciously mistreated
but I don't feel pain nor the blood in my mouth
just the bitterness of disloyalty.

Time goes by. Years, decades, centuries
but I am not ready to be found.

Slanders and hate on my name
I am a monster now, the most maligned monarch ever
Richard the murderer, the hunchbacked king.

I lay here in the dark.
I can hear the monks' choir, the horses' hooves
the carriages' wheels, the roar of iron lions upon me
but I am not ready yet.

Finally, my day arises.
It's the same day I was hidden from the world
the day they stopped looking at my abused body
and put an unnamed gravestone on what remained of me.

Today, I will rise again!
I have chosen my rescuer who will bring me back to life.
No clash of swords and halberds
just the mercy of all those who love me, who trust me
who still fight on my side, the ones I chose for my rebirth.
The White Rose of the Boar will blossom once again
for them.

Maria Grazia Lucrezia Leotta was born in Italy and graduated in Modern Foreign Languages and Literature. Eight years ago, thank to a bursary from the University of Sheffield, she moved to England with her family and she took an MA in Translation Studies. She fell in love with York and she recently moved there. She is an interpreter and a translator, a member of the Richard III Society and of the research for the Missing Princes Project for Philippa Langley who successfully led the search to locate King Richard's III grave.

Syeda Rumana Mehdi

Snow angel

A silent whisper
a single maple leaf
blows across the
threshold.

The drying roses
stand ajar
slightly apart
in the transparent vase.

Your footsteps are
still visible
on the dust coated
cascading staircase.

My life,
a sand particle
in an hourglass
falling through.

Trapped in a snowglobe,
snowflakes in my hair
twirling in a red dress
Still waiting for you.

Syeda Rumana Mehdi is a post graduate student studying Women's and Gender Studies at University of York. She is the author of "My Peace Poems" and "Lilies, Gunpowder and Dreams" and has been featured in "Vermont's Best Emerging Poets" for the last two years. She believes that poetry is her way of giving back to this world and that each verse is special and unique and finds a place in someone's heart.

Carole Meikle

What makes a poet?

The words that bubble from our souls
The pauses of reflection.
The phrases running in our heads like streams
That need to find the river.
The thinking and waiting and worry
About the vacuum
Then, a spark of inspiration
That comes from – where?
Hard, hard work, but then we have
An everlasting view and vision
That inspires the hearer and the reader
To take such deep breaths of awe
And to remember how we felt
When we first saw, heard or read it.

In tribute to Ana Lisa de Jong NZ and Mandana Ghonyloo

Carole Meikle has been a writer of inane doggerel for most of her life. But in autumn 2019 a few days spent with a friend who is a poet has stirred her into verse. She is so far un-published.

Alexandra M. Paun

@the Bombed Out Church

the Helping Hands
show up at 18:00
on the dot
& all the homeless people that have been waiting for the
past hour
get a free snack
a slice of pizza
a hot meal and a bread roll
then tea or coffee &
desert
so they can feel like normal people
having tea
they share the scraps
with the crippled pigeons &
the greedy seagulls & their babies &
after all have had their fill
the ants come out to clean up
the crumbs, the leftovers &
the drunk man's vomit

Alexandra M. Paun was born in Romania over 3 decades ago, and started writing poetry just 8 years later. Having journalism and scriptwriting as major life and writing experience, she's dedicated herself to literature in the recent years. She's been living in the UK for the past 2 years, and has just celebrated 14 months since she became a Yorkshire foster poet.

Lucy Pettigrew

York at Christmas

It's 3am and we are stumbling through the snowy streets
of York,
shuffling down snickleways and somehow ending up back
where we started.
We stop at the burger van for food to eat on the way home
and the HSBC cash machine for 'just-in-case' money,
letting the festivity emitting from the lights envelope us.
The Christmas tree next to the M&S
(that we've spent too many times sheltering from the
rain in)
looks too big for our drunk minds to comprehend so we
bypass it
in a flurry of laughter
and too many vodka-lemonades.

Letting the feeling of our warm flat guide us home
we find our way out of the maze of streets and walk along
the river because the main gate is locked at 11pm sharp
every night.
The flakes of snow start to make a home on our eyelashes
and our clothes

that are definitely not keeping us warm enough in this
minus-degree weather.
We stop again
and again
and again
to belly-laugh at throwaway jokes we won't remember
tomorrow daytime
and despite our physically freezing bodies we start to feel
warm in the glow of each other.

And, after all that,
when I'm safely tucked up in bed and thawing,
instead of feeling tired I feel awake,
and I can't wait to go out in the morning
and do it all over again.

Lucy Pettigrew is currently in her third year studying English Literature at York St. John University. She has been writing poems since the age of sixteen and self-published her debut poetry collection, The Light Within, in December 2018.

Georgina Petty

I Haven't Forgotten

Written and performed at Grandad's Funeral.

I Haven't Forgotten
You gently grip my hand
But you really don't understand
Never mind
Time may not have been kind
But let me go down memory lane
And remember once again
Even if you cannot
I have not forgot
Pick up a fircone and kick up the stones
The days before Ipads and mobile phones
Muddy walks with the dog
Swim with him against a sea of mind fog
Your lovely old Ben the smelly old hound
Underneath the table he could be found
Passing wind
Yet everyone else thought Dad had sinned
Knobbly knees
Climbing trees

Play once more an off key chopsticks tune
Or croakingly croon
Spanish Eyes
Looking up to the skies
I'm reminded feathered friends are your foes
Although
You've always enjoyed having a cat on your lap
Together with ex street cat Stanley you'd nap
Scrabble games
Forgetting names
Custard creams
Dozing off to dream
Of a golfing win
Sneakily opening up another tin

Of clotted cream fudge
Yet you never held a grudge
Against a hard day's toil
As the kettle would boil
You planted runner beans and grew tomatoes
All sorts grows
In the garden tended with care
The freshly ironed shirts you'd wear
Well worked hands gripped wood and steel
Provided for every home cooked meal
Whether down at the dairy or heavy lifting
You'd do what was necessary to get things shifting
From Renault to Peugeot your cars were pristine

Not a spot was left unclean
Whistling
Tickling
Playing with me and Mr Fox
Fixing a clock
Adjusting the toy koala in the car mirror ahead
You'd enjoy reading Dick Francis crime thrillers in bed
A flutter on the horses...here and there
As you silently sit there
I offer a drink
Take a moment to think
As you look past me into yourself
I pick up the photo album on the shelf
Corfe castle in the sunshine
A train journey across Dorset coastline
You went to Leeds and met football heroes
Those
Were some days
To be remembered always
Putting together puzzles bit by bit

You would sit
Browsing the newspaper
Tearing off folded football coupons for later
Muddled mistakes?
Never mind...have a cake
Crosswords proved frustrating
Better not keep Grandma waiting

Always late

But your company was great

Tutting over the Daily Mail

Madcap family days out at Moors Valley Rail

Competitive card games over a shandy

If it's Christmas you'd be persuaded for brandy!

Pudding was never to be skipped

Over the road you nipped

For a paper to see what's on telly tonight

As that light

In your head appears to go out

I have no doubt

Somewhere these memories are floating around

Waiting to be found

Yet they are not lost to me

So I'll let you be

In our hearts and in our minds you are still here

For you I will keep the thoughts, sights, sounds, magical moments and memories near

---

Georgina is a former Creative Writing tutor, current Goole RSPCA Secretary, Boothferry Verses member and Venue Manager for Junction Theatre Goole

Ella Potter

Fly

Her soul is stained with your black ink,
These scars won't fade and haven't healed with time,
And still, she looks for a clearing
In this dark midnight sky,
Sometimes the smoke clears, and again it's back,
But one day, the tears will finally dry,
And she will see what love
Looks like for the first time.

You couldn't keep her in that cage,
You couldn't clip her wings and tell her lies,
You couldn't say fragile birds aren't meant to fly,
She wouldn't watch her life behind a rusty door
That was latched tight as her spirit slipped away.
All you could do was keep her in sight
Because beautiful creatures cannot be confined,
Her wings will grow and she'll find the sky.

Ella Potter is an 18-year-old girl from Harrogate, North Yorkshire. She suffers with anxiety, depression, and PTSD. To cope with these issues, she write poetry. 'Fly' is the poem she wrote a year after her traumatic experience.

Eden Power

I sit in you burning

The evening air
Under the smoke that draws the night

I'm born in this ash, but never lived before

The wood of the trees remembered
Summer days and maybe
More

Written in rings, and forests grow
Seasons and seasons more

Burned fingers, lick into the sky, claw at smoke rings

But the flames weep in the wood now, beating on
old doors

Animal and alone the flame rips through my flesh and dust

To find myself the same as wood
When green heart sits
Naked for the sky

Eden power is a 24 year old woman from East Riding of
Yorkshire. She tends to find it difficult and awkward to write
in third person. She works as a "chef" and likes to occasionally
write "poetry" in her spare time. She once attended Hull
University and studied Chemistry. She is the proud pet parent
of a three legged dog called tripod.

John Regan

The Birds Don't Care

The birds don't care that we're not there to hear their
tuneful song
They flit from tree in life carefree within their
feathery throng

The bees are blind, and they don't mind if we aren't
there to see
They kiss the flower and dance through bower in sunny
patch or tree

The tiny ant has feeling scant cares nought of how we fare
They build their homes beneath cold stones away from
human stare

All nature too with wondrous hue ignoring mankind's
plight
She carries on in glorious song, knowing nothing of
our fight

John Regan is a part-time author and poet from Middlesbrough, currently living in Stainton Village. He works full-time as a telecom engineer at Openreach. He has a long-standing love of the written word and poetry.

Jamie H Scrutton

Big Knickers Rule!

Doreen has heard, they have returned in Vogue
They are back to being cool
They may not be visually flattering in sense
But big knickers rule!

She can't be doing with all of this provacative lingerie
They are nothing but a strand o f string
They are only good for you "you know what"
And that is a needless fling

She would rather feel adequately serene
It is more than she can say for some
For women that want to feel fabulous
With material stuck up their bum!

They slide between the orophus
They make for an uncomfortable grind
There is always a policy of keeping your unmentionables
intact
And that is to be kind, to your behind

So ladies, nevermind trying to impress your fellers, or girls

You have to be kind to be cruel

They may not be visually flattering in sense

But by god don't big knickers rules!

Jamie is a Yorkshire based Artist specializing in Spoken Word with Animation. His work is inspired by observational life with a spec of humor, which he adapts in to whimsical Animations. He has screened these Animations at events such as London based platforms - "Kino" "Exploding Cinema" and "Properganda." Also, "Showroom Shorts" based in Sheffield. Jamie often performs a Live recital of these Animations at specific events, as well as performing stand alone Anecdotes at various events around the UK. He has headlined his animated sets at events such as "Stanza Extravaganza" based at The Artisan Gallery based in Torquay and "Big Poetry" based at The Blue Walnut cafe, also in Torquay.

Antony Stones

Too Much For Me

The susurine sea sang,
"You're too small and shallow for me,
cessation and submission
shall shape the days of thee."

The whorling wind wailed,
"You're too weak and worthless for me,
withering and wearisomeness
will be the whole of thee."

The blistering sun blazed,
"You're too bent and broken for me,
bitterness and belligerence
shall be the best of thee."

The empty shadow echoed,
"You're too equivocal for me,
erosion and evasion
will etch the edge of thee."

And I, head high, replied,

"You talk too much for me,
you may not judge my heart,
I was not made for thee."

Antony Stones is a poet and spoken word artist from York, after working in the ambulance service for ten years, he moved into primary care to work as an advanced practitioner. his work predominantly discusses mental health from both personal and professional perspectives, with the aim of encouraging conversation and addressing misconceptions.

Hannah Storm

Little Birds Featherless on My Knee

You always said it was a parent's role to protect their
children,
to hold their hands across the road, keep them back from
the cliff,
even if the view was the kind you couldn't miss.
As I grew, you watched me pick my path,
saw me falter at the fork between risk and reward.

You swallowed silence like a blade when I strode that
unfamiliar road.
Still you waited. Saw my wings silhouette the sun,
waved me on, goodbye, confident I could fly on my own
until winter brought me home,
my little birds featherless on my knee.

It's our job to protect, you say.
And I nod, feeling the fear you felt that day
when I ran towards the edge, when I gripped the sky.
It wasn't until I was out of view,
when you could no longer fight for me that I fell
from flight.

And now that I feel the point of the blade I'd wield to shield my own,
now I know your fear, tell you how I fell,
hear how you had to swallow your wingless words
carved hollow by the violence.
In their vacuum no room for sword or silence.

Hannah Storm began writing flash fiction, poetry and creative non-fiction after almost two decades travelling the world as a journalist. She writes to pay tribute to the people she has met and the places she has been and to process her own experiences. Her writing has been published widely online and in several anthologies. She recently won the I Must Be Off travel writing competition and has been long and short-listed for numerous writing competitions, including the Bath Flash Fiction Award, Flash 500 and the Retreat West Flash Fiction Award. She lives with her husband and two children and when she's not writing or doing her media work, she runs marathons as another form of catharsis.

Henry Arthur Thorpe

The Barrow Downs

In the hills there are mounds,
Where the dead kings lie
There hides such cursed
Treasures, bound in
The hillside, that
They kept in death,
That they keep, still,
Shambling about their graves.

Don't go to the barrow downs,
In search of ancient gold,
All there is is gloom,
Death-laden silverware,
Jewels made ghoulish
By avarice ages old,
Lich-things who
Rise at night
To clutch at half dust things.

There is an eerie fog,
Made of dead breath
That clings to the hills,

Round the resting place
Of those who keep
Covetous in sleep,
Greedy clouds
That make curiosity
Deadly.

Be wary, lest
A spirit take you
And you stay forever
In an ancient hoard
Clinging to a dead lord's
Treasure, as they look
Out through your living eyes,
Until you too are dust.

When you travel through
The hillside tombs
Sing a song,
To while away the time,
The silence will come,
In the quiet come whispers
Whistle, so you don't listen,
Though if you pass the dancers
Do not join them.

It's best to leave the barrows be,
In their ever eerie fog,
It's best to leave the dead alone,
To their ancient restlessness,
Maybe take the longer path,
If you want to see another day.

Henry is a York based poet, originally from Somerset. He writes 'folky poetry', about myths, the countryside, the sea, magic and monsters. He has been around the York open mic poetry scene for a few years now, as co-host of BeSpeak and a regular at The Spoken Word. He has previously been published in the Looking Glass Anthology and Three Drops from a Cauldron. He enjoys walks in the woods, lore and mythology.

Elizabeth Walker

Learning to love yourself.

It's not an easy thing to do
When you've spent your whole life beating yourself black an
blue
Scolding yourself for not been good enough
Believing you'll never be enough to love
You have to believe these were never your thoughts
They were put in your head from all different sorts
People that never knew any better
How could they teach you something they never knew them-
selves
So nows the time to turn it around
Flip that coin and start living proud
Learn that your always more than enough
Your special and you'll always be loved
Stand in the mirror every morning you wake
Look at that gorgeous beautiful face
You won't find this love from anyone else
Not until you wake up and see it for yourself
When your so use to been told your not enough
Your always wrong and your to hard to love
Wipe that stuff right out your mind

That's not true it was told to you by the wrong kind
You are the one who puts out your worth
So step up your value
Don't put yourself down
Gather your strength and straighten that crown
Stand in that mirror every morning you wake and tell yourself
"I love you and I'm always proud",
"Your beautiful and strong and your not always wrong"
You have to see it and believe it for yourself
Before you can expect from anyone else
Once you learn to love yourself
You'll never feel needy to hear it from anyone else
You'll stop accepting less than you deserve
You'll raise the bar and realise your own worth
It's so important to love yourself
This inside work can't be done by anyone else
Once you love and see your own worth It'll be seen by all who
walk on this earth

Elizabeth Walker is a 46 year old mum from North Yorkshire, England. She is a self employed Reiki and Shamanic Practitioner. Elizabeth's aim in life is to help people find their way back to wellness through healing themselves and learning to love themselves.

Ian Whiteley

Cycle Of The Scarecrow

A scarecrow in autumnal sheen
thinks of all that he has been.
His age old frame begins to lean
as bitter winds blow in, so keen.
He longs for days of evergreen,
so buys back time, wipes the slate clean,
gives his soul to the pumpkin queen -
the witch who walks at Halloween.

The scarecrow dreams of living free
He thinks he's gonna survive
The summer sun, the winter snow,
He's never felt so alive.
The scarecrow dreams of living free
He thinks he's gonna survive
The springtime thaw, the autumn leaves,
He's never felt so alive.

A scarecrow in the wax moonlight
is snowed upon one winters night
and as the crystals, soft, alight

he dreams perhaps some day he might
take footsteps off into the bright
ice world. His skeletal delight
some hours later, fat and white
with snow-flesh - waiting for coal sight.

The scarecrow dreams of leaving home
He thinks he's gonna survive
The summer sun, the winter snow,
He's never felt so alive.
The scarecrow dreams of leaving home
He thinks he's gonna survive
The springtime thaw, the autumn leaves,
He's never felt so alive.

A scarecrow in a cutting rain
watches his slush slide down the drain
and as it leaves, he feels the pain
as bones of wood protrude and drain.
Weak sunlight sows the sleeping grain
as he is called upon, again,
to stand guard over crops – attain
dominance over winters stain.

The scarecrow dreams of working hard
He thinks he's gonna survive
The summer sun, the winter snow,
He's never felt so alive.

The scarecrow dreams of working hard
He thinks he's gonna survive
The springtime thaw, the autumn leaves,
He's never felt so alive.

A scarecrow dries in summer sun
knowing that, once more, he's won
the right of those, which he is one,
to face the crows of Albion.
Then as the solstice webs are spun
and shadows lengthen, day is done –
he knows that he cannot outrun
what summers beetles have begun.

The scarecrow dreams of dying now
He's not so sure he'll survive
The summer sun, the winter snow,
He's never felt less alive.
The scarecrow dreams of dying now
He's not so sure he'll survive
The springtime thaw, the autumn leaves,
He's never felt less alive.

A scarecrow in autumnal sheen
thinks of all that he has been.
His age old frame begins to lean
as bitter winds blow in, so keen.
He longs for days of evergreen,

so buys back time, wipes the slate clean,
gives his soul to the pumpkin queen -
the witch who walks at Halloween.

In Whiteley is a poet and singer/songwriter from Wakefield.
He publishes music under his project THE CROWS OF
ALBION and is a quarter of the performance group BARD
COMPANY. He hosts poetry open mic nights in both Wigan
(Write Out Loud, Wigan, Old Courts) and Wakefield (Getting
Gobby In The Lobby) and is a big fan of Wakefield Trinity
RLFC, despite currently residing in Wigan. He can be contact-
ed at his website: https://www.thecrowsofalbion.com/

About the Editor

James P. Wagner (Ishwa) is an editor, publisher, award-winning fiction writer, essayist, historian performance poet, and alum twice over (BA & MALS) of Dowling College. He is the publisher for Local Gems Poetry Press and the Senior Founder and President of the Bards Initiative. He is also the founder and Grand Laureate of Bards Against Hunger, a series of poetry readings and anthologies dedicated to gathering food for local pantries that operates in over a dozen states. His most recent individual collection of poetry is *Everyday Alchemy.* He was the Long Island, NY National Beat Poet Laureate from 2017-2019. He was the Walt Whitman Bicentennial Convention Chairman and teaches poetry workshops at the Walt Whitman Birthplace State Historic Site. James has edited over 60 poetry anthologies and hosted book launch events up and down the East Coast. He was recently named the United States Beat Poet Laureate for 2020-2021.

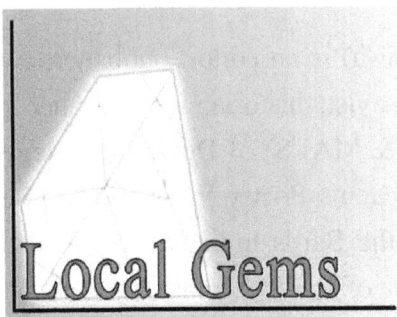

Made in the USA
Middletown, DE
25 October 2020